With warm thoughts and loving memories

To Grandma

From

Amanda, Mackenzie & Justin

Grandmother

new seasons™

a division of Publications International, Ltd.

Art Resource: Fine Art Photographic Library, London; Image Select;
Bridgeman Art Library, London/New York: *Grandmother Reading to Children* by Mary Cassatt,
Private Collection, New York; *Reading Le Figaro* by Mary Cassatt, Christie's Images,
London; *A Windy Day* by Liz Wright, Private Collection; **Sharon Broutzas; Marty Noble;**
Planet Art; Sacco Productions Limited, Chicago; SuperStock: Bradford City Art Gallery &
Museum, England/Bridgeman Art Library, London/New York; Christie's Images;
David David Gallery, Philadelphia; Armand Hammer Foundation, Los Angeles;
Huntington Library, Art Collections and Botanical Gardens, San Marino;
Private Collection/GG Kopilak; Museo Civico de Nittis,
Barletta/Canali PhotoBank, Milan; Private Collection/Daniel Nevins;
Brian Warling Photography.

Original inspirations by:
Lain Chroust Ehmann
Jan Goldberg
Marie Jones
Donna Shryer
Tricia Toney

Compiled inspirations by Joan Loshek

Grandmothers fill a special role
in the lives of their grandchildren.
They offer advice without an agenda,
attention without distraction,
and love without hesitation.

Look to grandmas for
a little extra help,
a little extra nudge,
a little more advice,
and a lot of extra love.

Grandmothers are the preservers of the past,

the caretakers of the present,

and the oracles of the future.

Grandmothers possess an incredible stamina
gained from long years of loving family and friends,
countless hours spent learning new things, and decades
of giving to others instead of to themselves.

A grandmother's kiss is soft

but filled with love.

A grandmother's hug is gentle

but filled with strength.

A grandmother's advice is simple

but filled with wisdom.

Listen to the words of those who are older,
for they have already fought and won the wars.

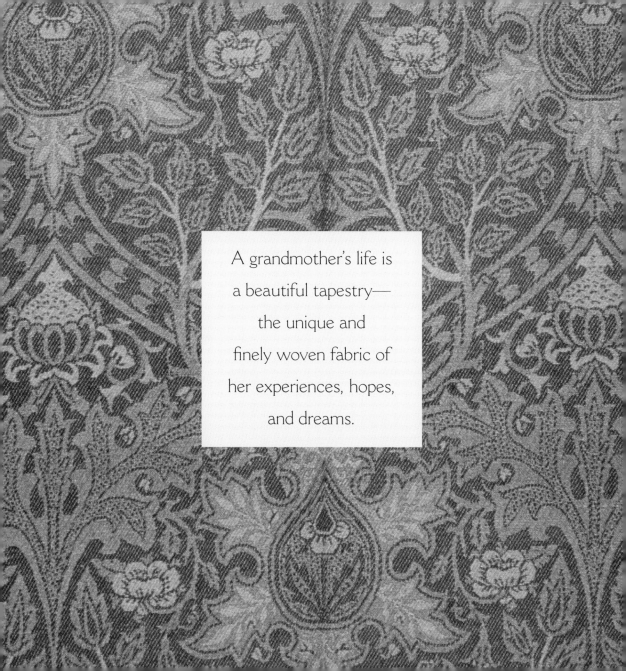

A grandmother's life is
a beautiful tapestry—
the unique and
finely woven fabric of
her experiences, hopes,
and dreams.

We turn no older with years, but newer every day.

EMILY DICKINSON

Grandma looks more beautiful now

than she did when she was my age.

When Grandmother
was a young woman,
she developed her
own powerful beauty
aids: courage, resolve,
poise, and integrity.

Today I will hold my grandmother's hand and enjoy a walk
down memory lane, for the passion in her tales is better
than that in any book on any library shelf.

Grandma gives to me a part of all that she has met in her life. She hands me courage to encounter strangers. She shows me compassion for those that are hurting. She lends me grace when people are rude. She gives me love whenever I may need it.

$\mathcal{L}$earning how to be a grandmother
is one of life's most enjoyable tasks:
You must accept the fact that you will
always be covered in kisses, asked to
care for baby grandchildren only
occasionally, and told repeatedly that
you are "The Best."

Everyone has two ages: chronological and spiritual.
The first dictates looks and physical activities. The
second fosters passion. When you allow your spiritual
age to dominate, you'll remain forever young at heart.

A grandmother
has a perspective of
family history that
no one else has.
Ask her about it,
then treasure and
preserve it.

As you grow older, learn to appreciate your grandmother. Love her sense of humor, her endless stories about "the way things used to be," and the wealth of knowledge that she gained from the passage of time and the overcoming of trials. Value the time you take to get to know her. Her connection with the past is priceless.

Grandmothers are like antiques:

Timeworn.

Precious.

Priceless.

Unique.

Grandma's presence makes reaching

milestones more meaningful.

Take satisfaction from what you have accomplished;

don't dwell on what you have yet to conquer.

Grandchildren and grandmothers
renew each other's spirits.

Our photo

My Grandma _____ and I like
to _____ together.

Grandmas know that memories are
the foundation upon which
our family's future is built.

Happiness is a warm pan of double-fudge brownies,

a cold glass of milk, and one of Grandma's stories.

Life Span

Maiden, mother, elder.

A grandmother's life matures.

Dawn, dusk, night.

A grandmother's dreams take flight.

Calm, wind, storm.

A grandmother's wisdom forms.

Beginning, middle, end.

On grandmother's love depend.

The seasons have meaning
     with Grandma.
In spring, we weed the beds and
     plant the flowers.
In fall, we pick the peaches, apples,
     and berries, canning and
     preserving their abundant
     sweetness.
In winter, we bundle up in afghans
     before the fire, reading, sharing,
     and laughing, while hot stew
     simmers on the stove.
When spring returns, daffodil bulbs
     poke up their shoots through
     softening earth.
And through every season,
     Grandma's love for us grows.

As a wife, I learned to love another human being with all his faults and frailties. As a mother, I learned to love without receiving anything in return. As a grandmother, I have learned to love unconditionally, without expectations and without limits. It is now that I see the boundless nature of love.

As a parent, I felt my job was to teach my children all I knew about life. Now, as a grandmother, my job is to tell my grandchildren what I *don't* know so we can learn it together.

Making it through each day takes fortitude.

Making it through nearly an entire century

requires sheer brilliance.

A reassuring nod.

An encouraging phrase.

A wealth of wisdom.

Unending praise.

A meaningful hug.

A joke shared by two.

A tender moment,

just Grandma and you.

Intelligence can be measured by certificates on your wall or books you have read, but, in the end, all of that knowledge pales in comparison to the wisdom gained when you truly participate in life.

No matter how big a family
grows, grandmas recognize
the uniqueness of every member.
Each grandchild has a different
personality, a special blend of
character, and a little piece
of Grandma in him.

The warmth of a
genuine hug
can send the
spirit soaring.

Today I will call my grandmother
and tell her how much I love her.

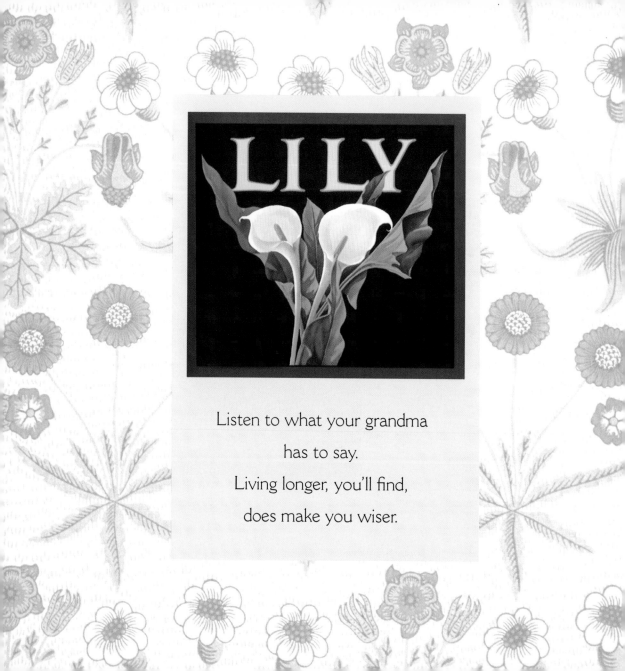

LILY

Listen to what your grandma
has to say.
Living longer, you'll find,
does make you wiser.

Grandmother's devotion to
her family ensures she's
never far from its heart.

When I ask my grandmother what to do,
she tells me to look in my heart.
When I ask her where I need to go,
she tells me to search my soul.
What I love most about my grandmother
is how she teaches me not with worldly words
of wisdom but by gently reminding me
of the simple truths that I already know.

Today we scrutinize, analyze, and
departmentalize until problems are
pulverized. Sometimes, in this rushed,
mad world, we should stop and do things
Grandma's way: Wait, watch, and listen
until solutions naturally evolve.

Our photo

At Grandma's house, everyone feels at home.

Sleep at Grandma's house is sweet slumber, always secure.

The glow of the night-light reassures you.

The soft tick of the mantel clock soothes you.

The constant warmth from the furnace comforts you.

And Grandma's love surrounds you.

Grandma knows that
enough love is
never really enough.
She'll always offer more.

Grandmother's smile is a silent song,
her laughter a fun surprise,
but nothing fills my heart with joy
like the love in Grandmother's eyes.

Grandma's always there,

no matter how you fare,

to provide support

and share

in all of your endeavors.

Grandma has good memories,

she tells us often,

of love and life,

of joys she's seen,

of wonders we'll behold someday.

When I'm with my grandma

the world becomes new,

an adventure once again.

No matter what grandmas look like
or what makes them stand apart,
there is no greater treasure
than a grandma's
loving
heart.

Inner beauty never grows old.

When I love my grandchild,

I hold dear my husband, my own children,

and myself all at once,

for pieces of each of us reside

in this miraculous child.

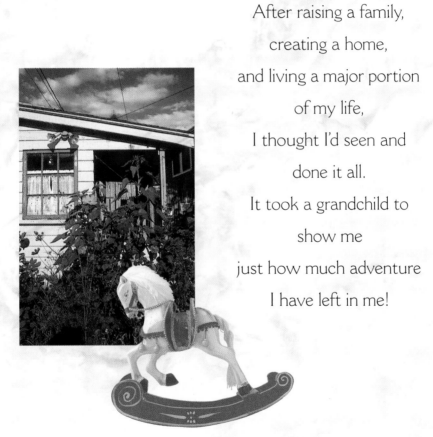

After raising a family,

creating a home,

and living a major portion

of my life,

I thought I'd seen and

done it all.

It took a grandchild to

show me

just how much adventure

I have left in me!

The faint scent of
Grandma's perfume, her
hair, her lipstick, all stay
with us throughout our
lives, bringing a smile
and a warm feeling
each time we
remember.

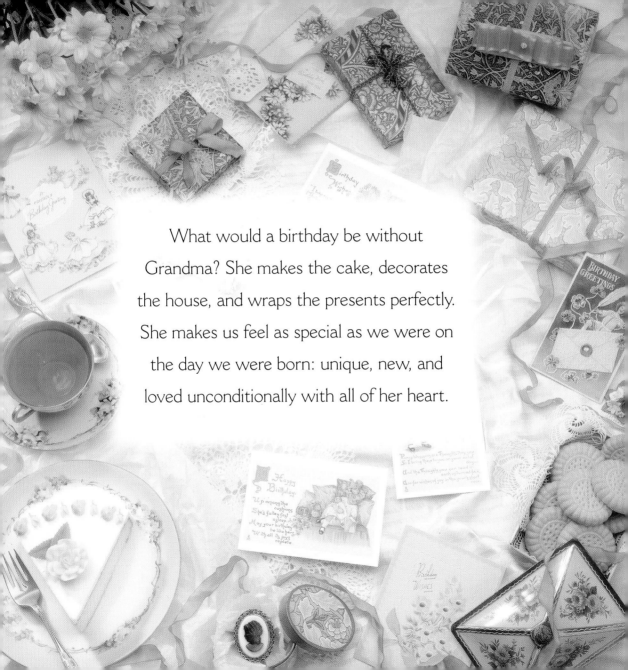

What would a birthday be without Grandma? She makes the cake, decorates the house, and wraps the presents perfectly. She makes us feel as special as we were on the day we were born: unique, new, and loved unconditionally with all of her heart.

At a moment's
notice, a grandma
will willingly provide
a haven where you
can go to emotionally
recover from the
trials of the day.

Photo

Every day with Grandma is a holiday.

*W*hen I look into my grandmother's face,
I see satisfaction not with the possessions she owns
but with the lives she has touched while raising my
wonderful mother, nurturing me, and now
bringing my own daughter to gleeful smiles by
simply opening her arms in love.

A grandmother's face is

a map of her life.

Each fine line represents a path

traversed with joy, a journey

undertaken with courage, a road

traveled upon with love.

Love blooms like a rose garden in Grandma's heart.
The whole family marvels at the strength of the roots,
the length of the stems, and the beauty of the blossoms.

Rosa lutea maxima flore pleno

Rosa provincialis flore in carto pleno.

Rosa centifolia rubra.

Rosa prænestina variegata.

My grandma tells me to love always,

that love is handed down through the years,

that love conquers all.

Grandmothers are so special,

each child is blessed to have more than one.